S·T·A·R·T·I·N·G
Zele Lace

S·T·A·R·T·I·N·G
Zele Lace

AGNES STEVENS
with IVY RICHARDSON

Dryad Press Ltd, London

© Agnes Stevens 1989
First published 1989

ISBN 0 85219 793 4

Typeset in Garamond by Tradespools Ltd., Frome, Somerset
and printed in Great Britain by Anchor Press Ltd, Tiptree, Essex
for the Publishers
Dryad Press Ltd
4 Fitzhardinge Street
London W1H 0AH

A CIP record for this book is available from the British Library

Preface

When I received a letter from Dryad Press asking me to
write a book on needlelace, I was pleasantly surprised.
Although I have made needlelace for over 12 years, I had
never thought of writing such a book. The constant
encouragement of Mrs Susan Cox of The English Lace
School eventually convinced me I ought to try: my most
sincere thanks to her.

I also want to thank my husband and my children,
especially Jenny, for their invaluable assistance in
translating and typing, and for their encouragement. For
their continuing interest which has made me understand
the need to record techniques, I thank my many wonderful
pupils. My thanks also to Mrs Ivy Richardson for her
editing and proof-reading.

I hope that this book will provide a firm foundation for
anyone who wishes to learn this ancient art form.

It is my greatest wish that, through your hands, many
English homes will soon display beautiful Zele needlelace.

Agnes Stevens   December 1988

Explanatory notes

Some of the terms used in this book will not be familiar to English lacemakers. This explanatory note will help to make them clear.

'Flat work' is simple buttonhole stitch – not twisted
'English gaas' is twisted buttonhole stitch
'Traceren' is laying down the cordonet
'Klitsen' are connecting buttonholed bars, often worked in a regular pattern, i.e. squares, hexagons, three-pronged forks, or singly. They are never couched down – they are worked over three threads.
'Legs' are picots, usually elongated in Zele lace, and used to embellish and decorate the outer edges of needlelace, and klitsen, also worked over three threads. A back stitch keeps them in place, making them easier to work and keeping an overall even length
'Making a connection' means joining one part of the pattern to another while couching, or, when making the klitsen and legs, by looping one of the double thick threads over the part of the traceren where the join is to be and stretching it back to the other if it occurs during the traceren; or by looping the single thread needed when making "legs" or "klitsen" into the back stitch made for the specific purpose of fixing them in place
'Klare stitches' are open stitches
A noose is what we call a loop.

Ivy Richardson

Contents

O•N•E
Introduction

Materials
- a pattern
- blue wrapping-paper
- two layers of cotton fabric, approximately 4 cm bigger than the pattern
- self-adhesive transparent matt vinyl
- needles no. 10 and no. 8
- very fine fragile cotton thread no. 100/2 or 120/2
- cotton thread no. 24/3
- a thimble
- a pair of scissors with fine points

Making the pattern ready to work
1. Transfer the pattern to the blue paper, by using white carbon paper
2. Cut the pattern out of the blue paper, leaving approximately 2 cm around the edge
3. To strengthen the blue pattern, stick the self-adhesive matt transparent plastic to the pattern
4. The strengthened pattern is tacked on a double layer of cotton fabric approximately 1 cm from the outside of the pattern line

The successive workings:
1. The traceren – make the legs – make the 'klitsen'
2. The first filling : flatwork
3. The second filling : English gaas
4. The embroidery

The terms we use in England for these stages:
1. Laying the cordonet – making the picots – making the inter-connecting framework of bars
2. The first filling : corded buttonhole stitch
3. The second filling : twisted buttonhole stitch
4. Padding the outline and finishing with buttonhole stitch

T•W•O
What is traceren?

Traceren is outlining the basic line of the needlelace on top of the pattern by means of two strong threads. These are fastened on top of the patternline with a very fine fragile thread. This is the only thread which goes through both the pattern and the double layer of fabric.

When the work is completely finished, the double layer of fabric will be torn apart, so that this fine thread breaks. The needlelace is then completely free of the pattern and it is very easy to pick the little threads out of the work. *Never cut open* the double layer of fabric with a pair of scissors: it is then very hard to pick out those little threads.

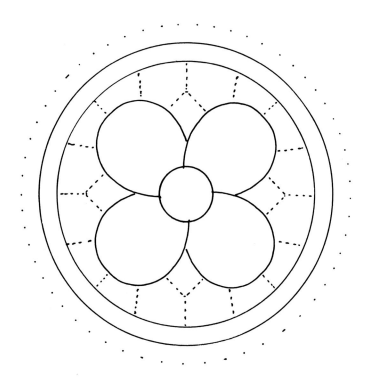

The filled lines are traceer lines.
The dotted lines are 'klitsen' and are **not** getraceerd (couched down).
The outside line is to fasten the legs (use a backstitch).

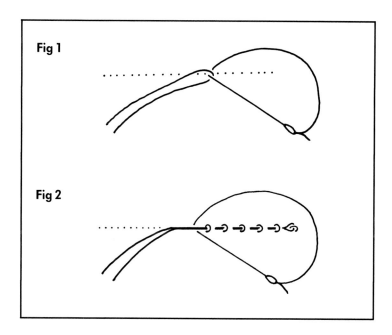

Fig 1

Fig 2

How to traceer   Take a strong thread (Brok no. 23/4 cord) approximately 2 m long and fold it in half. Make a loop with the double thread (see Fig 1). Thread a no. 10 needle with the very fine thread (no. 100/2). Fasten this very fine thread on the wrong side of the fabric. Stick the needle through the fabric and the paper on the pattern line as close as possible to the middle of the pattern.

Stitch with the needle over the loop and back into the same hole. Approximately 2 mm further along, stick the needle upwards, over the two strong threads and back again in the same hole (see Fig 2). Continue this way and follow the pattern line.

Caution: as you pull on the fine thread, *do not* pull the strong thread down. These two strong threads must lie along the pattern line.

Why do we always stitch the needle back into the same hole it comes out of?   When you stitch the needle through the fabric and the cloth, you must always go back through the same hole. In this way you can traceer in a strong and steady way. If you stick your needle back in another place, you will not have a firm basic line. Your work will be distorted. When the fine thread breaks, or you need another one, just fasten it off and restart on the underside, in the fabric, and make small stitches again.

You must always make sure that the parts of the pattern, where they meet, are connected, not just touching together; they must be joined to each other. In the rest of the section on couching and laying the cordonnet these points will be called 'connections'.

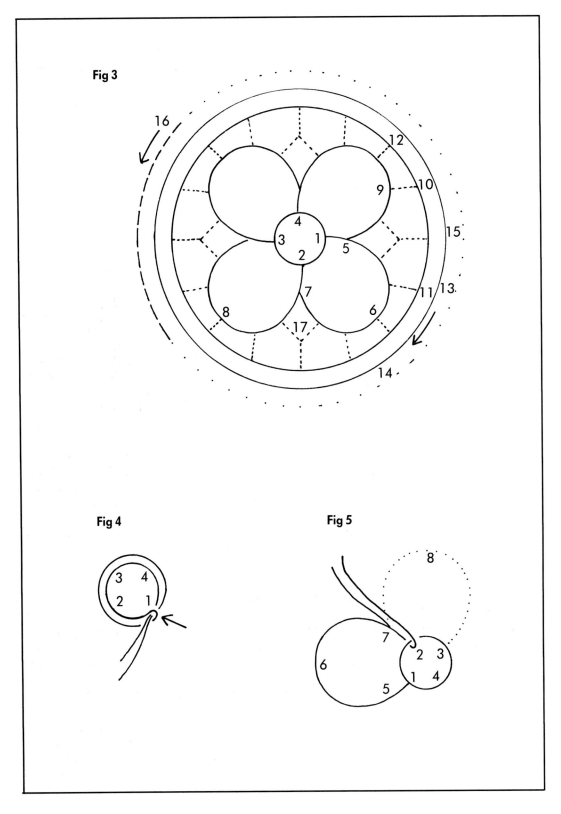

Fig 3

Fig 4

Fig 5

12

How to traceer the first pattern

Fasten the fine thread always at the back of the fabric. Follow the numbers in order when you traceer (Fig 3).

Start at 1 with a *closed noose* (see Fig 4). Leave the noose big enough and couch in the direction 2-3-4 back to 1. In this way you can always pull the strong thread. Couch further to 5-6-7.

Your first connection will be from 7 to 2 (Fig 5). Bring your couching thread and needle upwards at 2. Take one of the two strong outlining threads, push this thread under the traceerline of the circle and pull through. Fold the thread back to the waiting thread at 7. Couch from 2 to 7. Take the two threads together again and couch further to 8. Continue couching, making the connections as described, until you reach 9. From 9 with one thread to 5, make the connection and couch back from 5 to 9 and fasten with one extra stitch.

Bring your needle up at 10. Fasten the two threads at 10 and couch further from 10 to 11 until you reach 12. Do not couch from 12 to 10. Bring your needle to the top of your work at 10, make a connection at 10, fold the thread back and couch from 10 to 12. Cut the two strong threads and fasten the fine thread firmly in the fabric.

Start with an open noose at 13 (see the open noose in Fig 1) and couch further to 14 and 15. There, make a connection in the same way as for the first big circle between 12 and 10. With a double fine thread, make a backstitch at line 16. Every stitch is 0.6 cm in size and 0.5 cm away from the outer traceerline (Fig 3). These back stitches are supports for the long picots or legs on the outer edge. Also make a similar little stitch at every three-forked klits or framework (17 in Fig 3).

How to work the first pattern

Start every pattern with the long picots or legs.

What are legs? Legs are little projections made as extra decoration at the outside of a piece of needlelace. Make particular note of the action, the working and the holding of the needle. Take the couched pattern and lay it over the left forefinger so that the working part lies above the finger. Hold the pattern with the left thumb and ring finger. Hold the working thread gently with the middle finger.

After stretching three threads, hold the needle as if it were a cigarette in the right hand, between the fore and middle fingers. Push the needle through with the thumb. Always work away from yourself, and from left to right.

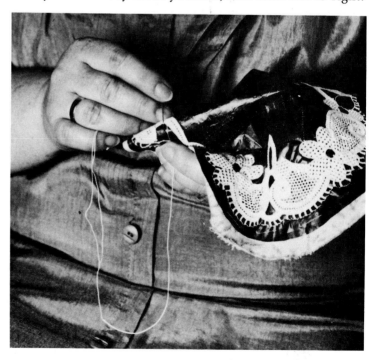

Photo 1: Here the action and working method are shown

14

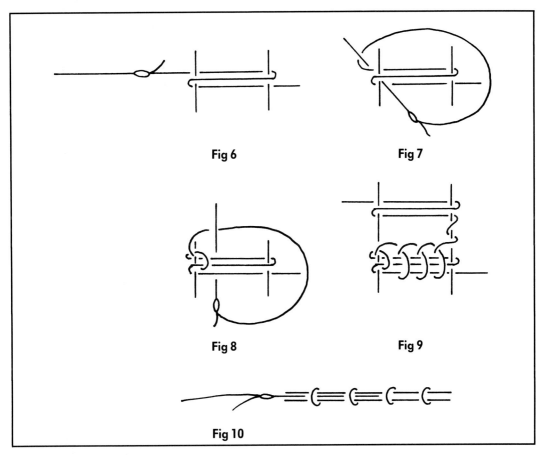

Fig 6

Fig 7

Fig 8

Fig 9

Fig 10

How to make legs Stretch three threads under the traceer line from right to left under the back stitch. Over the back stitch work from left to right, again under the traceer line and under the back stitch.

In this way, you make a foundation of three threads (Fig 6). Push the needle in the loop of the double thread and under the back stitch (Fig 7) (the thread automatically lies under the needle) and pull through. Thus we now have a little knot. In this way, the rest of the stitches can never slip away. Now continue with a flat stitch (Fig 8). Trap the thread from the little knot under the middle finger and keep it in position.

Push the needle under the three stretching threads between the back stitch and the first traceer line. The thread automatically lies under the needle. Pull the needle through. Make seven or more stitches. After the last stitch, move on to the next leg. Fasten once under the traceer line and connect securely.

At the next leg, stretch the thread again (Fig 9). To finish the thread, stick the needle several times into the traceer line (Fig 10).

15

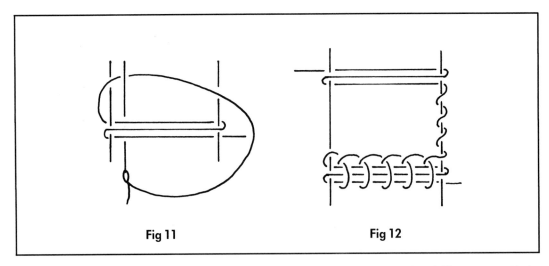

Fig 11   Fig 12

The klitsen Klitsen are the connections between the different motifs in needlelace.

How to make klitsen Stretch three threads from right to left and back between the motifs at the marked place. Make sure that you go completely under the couching thread (Fig 11) and work over three threads with a flat stitch (Fig 12).

This is the same action as for the legs, but without the first little knot. Make sure that every time you pull a stitch, you hold the thread under the middle finger. Do not place the stitches too close to each other, but pull them firmly. At the end of the bar, continue up to the next bar (Fig 9). Whip several times under the traceer line, according to the distance between the klitsen, and pull this thread evenly so that the thread forms one line with the traceer line.

The three-forked klits Fig 13 shows the unworked three-forked bars. Stretch the thread from 1 to 2, catch under the little stitch and on to 3 under the traceer line. Come above the traceer line and back under 2 to 4 under the traceer line. Work over the traceer line back under 2 and to 1 under the traceer line. Work over the traceer line back under 2 and to 4 under the traceer line. Work over the traceer line back under 2 to 1 under the traceer line (Fig 14). In this way, you will have four and two stretching threads. The needle shows the beginning of the flat stitch (Fig 15).

As you can see, Fig 15 lines in another direction: hold your work in the position shown. Start with a flat stitch from 1 to 2, work to the middle, stretch the working thread from 2 to 3 under the traceer line (Fig 16). Turn your work to the left. Work from 3 to 2. Pull the first stitch at 2 firmly so that you can hardly see it and work till 4 (Fig 17).

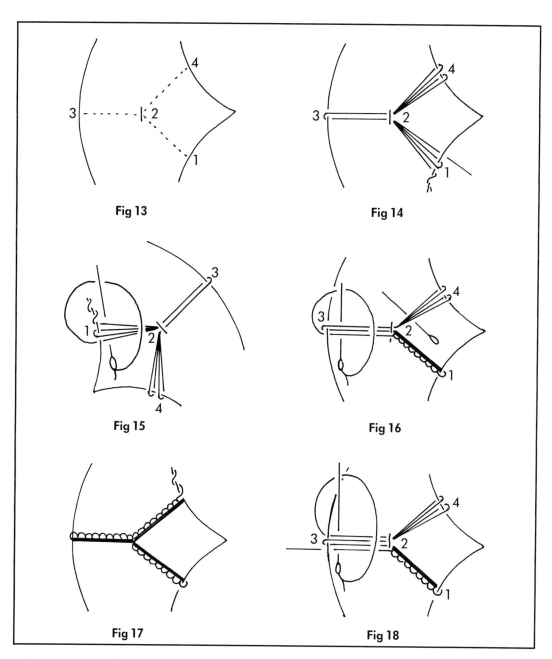

Fig 13

Fig 14

Fig 15

Fig 16

Fig 17

Fig 18

Starting and finishing a thread while making klitsen

Finish the thread, when the klits is completely worked, by pushing up into the traceer line. Cut the fastened thread as short as possible.

Start a new thread while forming the stretching threads. If you have started a three-forked klits and found that your thread is not long enough, it is best to start a new thread at 3. Leave the old thread hanging at this point, add the new thread at 3 from the inside to the outside and work across 4 threads (Fig 18).

The first filling: flatwork

What is flatwork?

1. Flatwork is the same stitch as is used for klitsen, but between every stitch there is an opening just big enough to put your needle through the next row
2. The stitches have to look like rounded squares. If you make rectangular stitches, then your work looks as if it has been stretched out, and that is wrong
3. *Never* use a thread longer than your arm
4. Never make knots in your thread to start
5. Always put the free end of the thread in your needle, *not* the part cut from the reel
6. Hold your work as described in *How to work the first pattern*
7. Pay particular attention to the action, holding and working of the needle
8. Always work from left to right and from the left side of the working area. Thus you never hold too much in your hand

Starting the thread

This is an explanation of how to work a square piece. Push the needle from the inside to the outside under the traceer thread at the left-hand side of the motif (Fig 19) and leave approximately 2 cm thread lying above the lowest traceer line. Put your thumb on that short end of thread (Fig 20).

Hold the working thread under your middle finger.

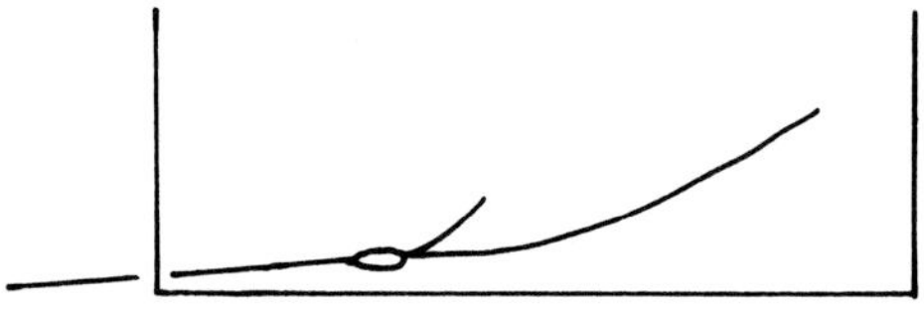

Fig 19

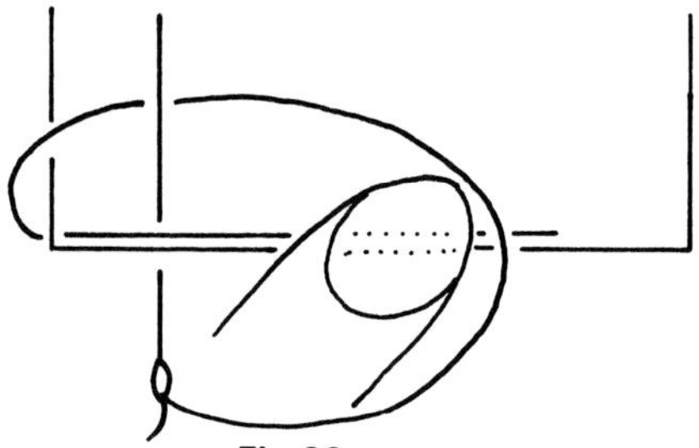

Fig 20

Push the needle under the bottom traceer line, 1 mm beyond the vertical traceer line. The thread automatically lies under the needle. Pull the needle through (Fig 21). (The distance between the stitches only applies when working with no. 24/3 cotton.)

At the end of the first row, push the needle from right to left under the traceer line, from the outside to the inside of the motif. Stretch the thread to the left and push under the traceer line from right to left or from the inside to the outside of the motif (Fig 22). English lacemakers call this 'laying a cord'.

Immediately pick up the first full space plus the stretching (cording) thread. Make one stitch in every space until the end of the row (Fig 23).

In this way you make a half space in the beginning of the row. At the end of the row you have to decide for yourself how big the last space will be. If you have a half space, do not make a stitch. If you have a full space or something more than a half space, make a stitch. Start the third row with a full stitch; make the first stitch in the first full space (see **x** in Fig 23).

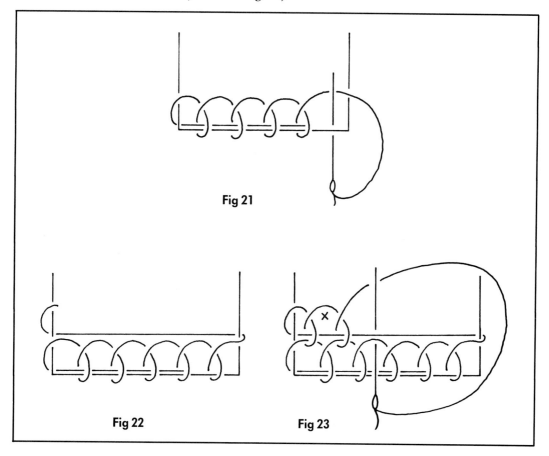

Fig 21

Fig 22

Fig 23

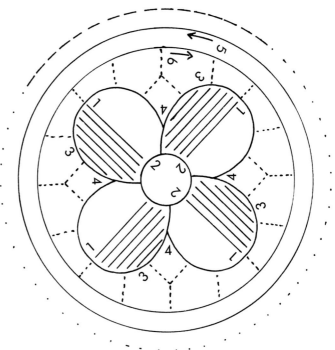

Fig 24

Working the first leaf of the motif with flatwork

As you can see this is a motif with curved lines, which has to be worked using horizontal lines.

First mark the middle of the section by scoring lightly on the vinyl with your needle. Do not go through the vinyl (see Fig 24 between **1** and **2**). Then mark out parallel horizontal lines downwards to the lower edge of the leaf. Thus you can see the direction of the work and where you have to start (see Fig 24 between **3** and **4**).

Start the thread at **3** (see Figs 19 and 20).

Remember that every stitch is 1 mm high and 1 mm wide. Make a horizontal line 1 mm above the deepest point of the traceer line. Use the needle as a guide. Push the needle in at the right side under the traceer line and under the traceer line at the left side (Fig 25). Thus you can see if your needle lies parallel with the middle line. The point at the left, where the needle touches the traceer line, is the starting point.

Push the needle under the traceer line at this point and make the first stitch 1 mm to the right over the traceer line and the working thread (Fig 26). Pull the first two stitches a little bit harder. Make normal stitches in the middle and pull the stitches at the end of the row a little bit harder.

This makes a horizontal line, but it is only for the first row. Stretch the thread in the same way as in Fig 22. The stretching thread lies on top of the first row of stitches.

Use your needle again as a guide to help to stretch your

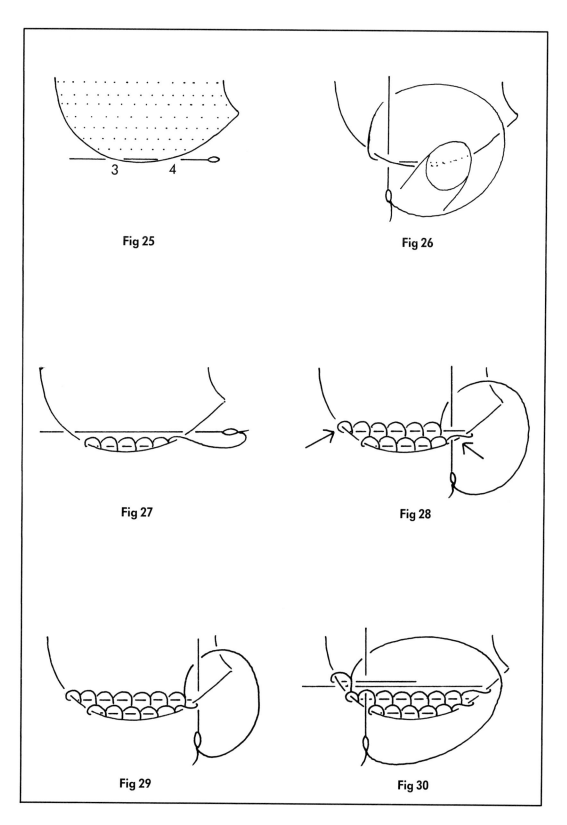

Fig 25

Fig 26

Fig 27

Fig 28

Fig 29

Fig 30

21

thread horizontal (Fig 27). Make the first stitch where the stretching thread crosses the traceer line. Make one or more stitches on the traceer line as you think necessary (see the arrow on Fig 28). Complete the row by making one stitch in every opening.

Pay particular attention at the end of every succeeding line. The noose which is formed by the thread which goes under the traceer line has to serve for one stitch (see the arrow on Fig 28). Only after this stitch can you make extra stitches on the traceer line (Fig 29).

It is important that you do not have spaces which are too big at the beginning and end of each row. Do not make the stitches too close. When your thread seems to be too short, do not work with it any longer. Your thread needs only to be as long as three times the length of the part you will have to work plus twice the length of the needle. Always start a new thread at the beginning of a row (Fig 30). If you look carefully at Fig 30, you can see that the old stretching thread is normally stretched and kept at the left side. Start a new thread working from the inside to the outside under the traceer line in the same place as the old stretching thread. Take these two threads along for approximately seven stitches. Be careful that the new thread does not show in your work. Finish this row and cut the old stretching thread as close as possible to the traceer line.

Work half of the motif until you reach the dotted line. Here you can make a little variation to bring some life to your work. This is called 'a row of open stitches'.

How to make a row of open stitches

Instead of stretching the thread, take your thread up through every other stitch (Fig 31) as far as the dotted line reaches. Stretch the thread further over the rest of the stitches till the end of the row (Fig 32).

Work the beginning of the next row with flat stitches until you reach the first stitch that you took up. Make a big loose flat stitch above in the stitch that you did not take up with your laid thread (Fig 33).

Work this row completely and stick your needle from the right to the left under the traceer line. Take up every big space instead of laying your thread, and lay the thread above the flat stitches (Fig 34).

Work the next row completely with flat stitches (Fig 35). Make two flat stitches in the large spaces. Make sure that you pull the first stitch a little bit to the left and the second stitch a little bit to the right. Continue flatwork until the motif is completely filled.

As the rows get shorter, you have to make fewer stitches. Work as follows:

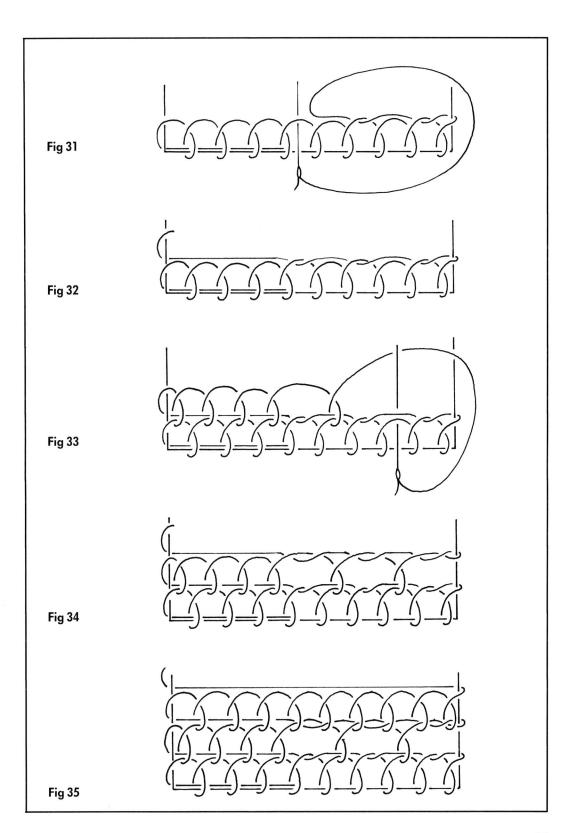

Fig 31

Fig 32

Fig 33

Fig 34

Fig 35

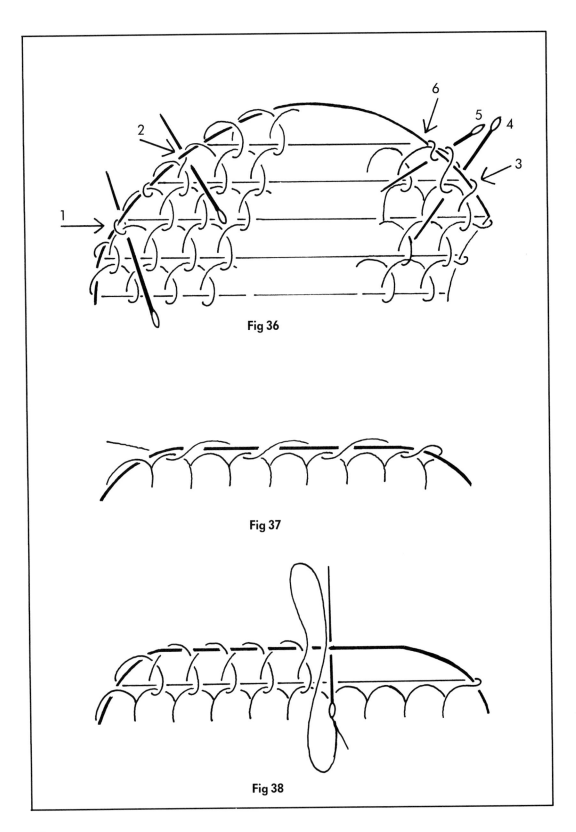

Fig 36

Fig 37

Fig 38

Handkerchief corner

Two complete flowers,
showing combination of petals
and leaves (worked by Agnes
Stevens)

Dove and initials motif

Very fine flower with two
leaves, to embellish a wedding
dress (worked by Agnes
Stevens)

This small flower is part of a
gold pendant (worked by
Agnes Stevens)

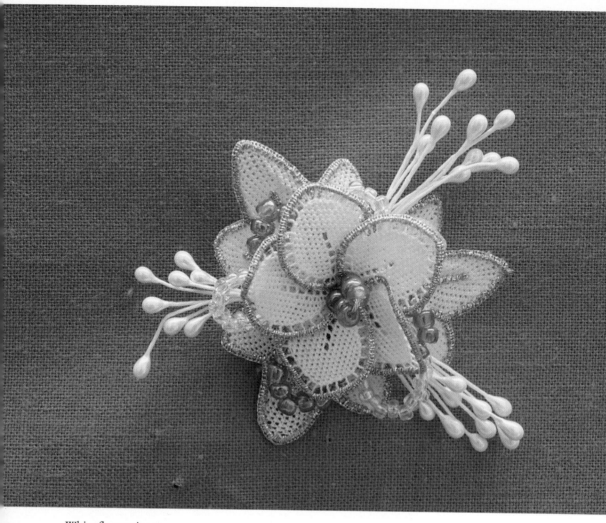

White flowerpiece,
embroidered with gold thread
and embellished with blue
pearls (worked by Agnes
Stevens)

Either: Lay a thread and start a new row of stitches. Sometimes miss the first space or push your needle in the first opening and then under the traceer line outwards so that this stitch is fastened, but is not a real stitch (Fig 36 needle and arrow **1**).

Or: Make the first stitch as usual but then stick the needle under the traceer line to the outside (Fig 36: needle and arrow **2**).

Work to the end of the row, then the last stitch is the stitch which connects to the traceer line. Lay the thread normally (Fig 36 arrow **3**) but make sure that all the end stitches of the row below are fastened at the traceer line. If not, then bring the needle from right to left under the traceer line and pick up the loose stitch (Fig 36, needle **4**). Go back over the traceer line in the last stitch (Fig 36, needle **5**) and lay the thread for the next row (Fig 36, arrow **6**).

To finish the last row

This can be worked in two ways:
1. When the last row is completely finished, push with your needle under the traceer line and pick up one stitch plus the traceer line. Do the same for every other stitch (Fig 37). After the last stitch cut the thread as short as possible, close against the traceer line.
2. When you start the last row of stitches, make a first stitch, pushing the needle under the traceer line and pulling through. Make the next stitch, then bring the needle under the traceer line and pull through (Fig 38). Fasten the thread at the end of the row beneath the traceer line.

The second filling: raised English gaas

What is raised English gaas?

This stitch consists of groups of two turned stitches which are made close to one another, and separated from the rest of the row by a big space. Instead of laying a thread across the top of the stitches, pick up the big space separating the pairs of twisted stitches.

To begin the next row of stitches, put your thread, through the traceren in the same way as with flatwork, but go once more upwards under the traceer line to achieve the necessary height (see the arrow in Fig 39). Every stitch is approximately 2 mm high and two stitches are approximately 2 mm wide. Every big space is approximately 2 mm wide. Start the first row with a space (Fig 39).

To make the stitch

The thread lies under the left middle finger. Push the needle up under the traceer line. Wind the thread (the part closest to the eye of the needle) around the needle from the right, under the needle, to the left, and from the left, above the needle, to the right and pull the needle through (see the needle in Fig 39). Make two stitches close to each other. Leave a space of approximately 2 mm and make two stitches.

At the end of the row, at the top of the stitches (see arrow in Fig 40) bring the needle from the right to the left under the traceer line and pick up every big space. This is instead of laying a thread along the top of the stitches as in flatwork (see needle in Fig 40). After picking up the last big opening, put your needle back in the opening and under the traceer line. Put the needle once more under the traceer line to achieve the necessary height. You only need to make the spaces in the first row. In succeeding rows, the spaces are formed automatically.

Work the second row as follows. Make the first stitch in the big space and pull this stitch to the left side. Make the second stitch next to the first stitch in the same way. The big spaces come automatically as you place your pairs of stitches in the big spaces picked up with the returning thread.

26

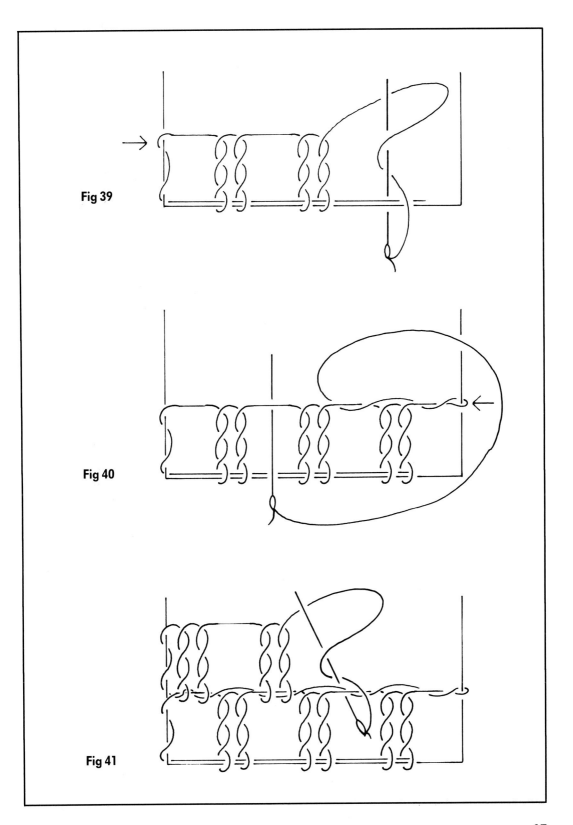

Fig 39

Fig 40

Fig 41

Some useful advice

You have to feel this stitch: you need to make long stitches. When you make a stitch, the thread glides over the paper and is pulling downwards. Tighten the space between one group of two stitches and the next by pulling the thread to the left (see needle in Fig 41). Place your middle finger on the thread immediately after pulling a stitch.

Filling up the second motif with raised English gaas

In this motif the outside line is curved. First mark the middle of the petal and then mark out every 2 mm with little horizontal lines. As you can see, the height between two horizontal lines is not the same at the beginning and at the end of a row: this means you *cannot* start with two twisted stitches.

Starting with a space, make two flat stitches, a space and then make two twisted stitches (Fig 42, arrow **1**) or start with a space and make one flat stitch and one turned stitch, a space and two turned stitches (Fig 42, arrow **2**).

Think of the corresponding area at the end of a row. In Fig 42, arrow **2**, you see a turned stitch and a flat stitch at the end of the row. These are all possibilities which you can use, but the line of the head of the stitches must be on the same *horizontal* line. Note that on the same line you have to cross the traceer line (Fig 42, arrow **3**).

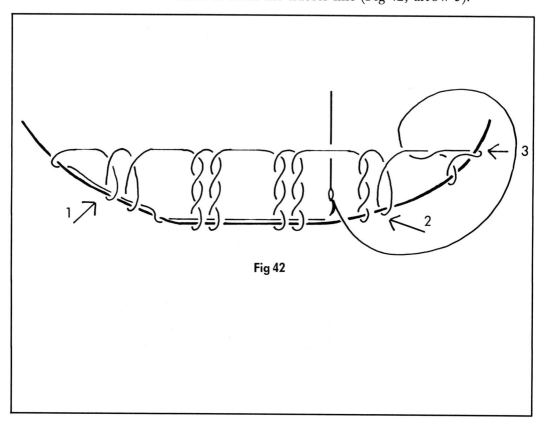

Fig 42

28

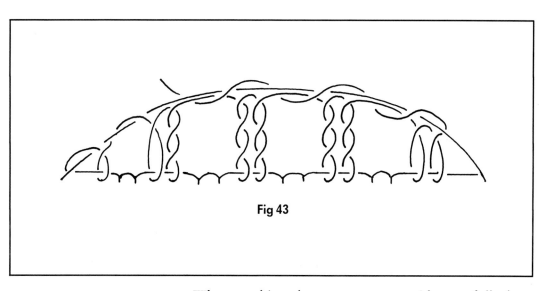

Fig 43

When working the next rows, consider carefully how you can begin and end (when to use flat stitches, etc.) to keep the row horizontal. Every row is different. Here are some more examples:

- start with one flat stitch, make a space, two flat stitches, a space and then two twisted stitches;
- start with one flat stitch, make a space and then two twisted stitches;
- start with one twisted stitch, make a space and then two twisted stitches.

When the rows are getting smaller, you can use the same method as in Fig 36. But look carefully to see which combinations you can use to begin and to end your rows.

Fasten all the big spaces at the traceer line in the last row (Fig 43) and cut the thread very close after the last stitch.

S•I•X

How to work the big circle

This circle is filled with flatwork. Start at 5 (see Fig 24) at the inside of the line with legs and work from the left to the right (see the arrow in Fig 24). Make the flat stitches a little bit bigger than normal, but not too big, otherwise it looks like a row of klare stitches, which is not correct. Take into account that the more rows you make, the closer the stitches will become.

When your thread is too short for the first row, start a new thread as follows: lay the old thread near the traceer line. Bring your needle with the new thread through the last stitch from the back to the front (see Fig 44, needle 1).

Work further over the traceer line and the two threads (see Fig 44, needle **2** and Fig 45). At the end of the first row you have to make a connection as follows: put your needle in the first stitch and pull through (Fig 46).

Use a separate thread as stretching thread (Fig 47, arrow 1) above the stitches. Make the first stitch of the second row in the same stitch as your connection (Fig 47, arrow **2**).

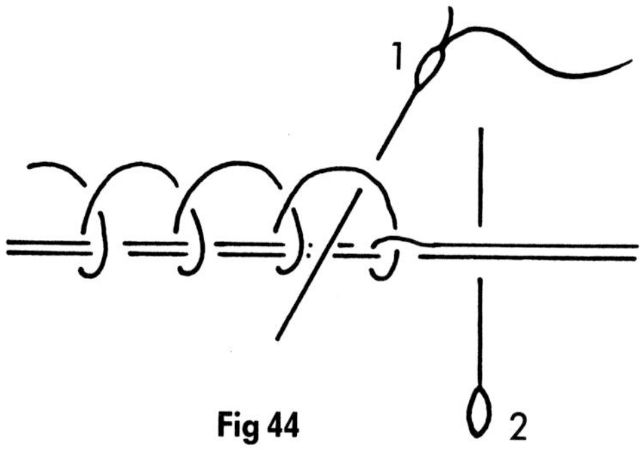

Fig 44 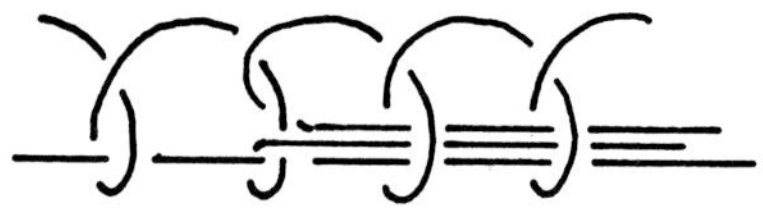 **Fig 45**

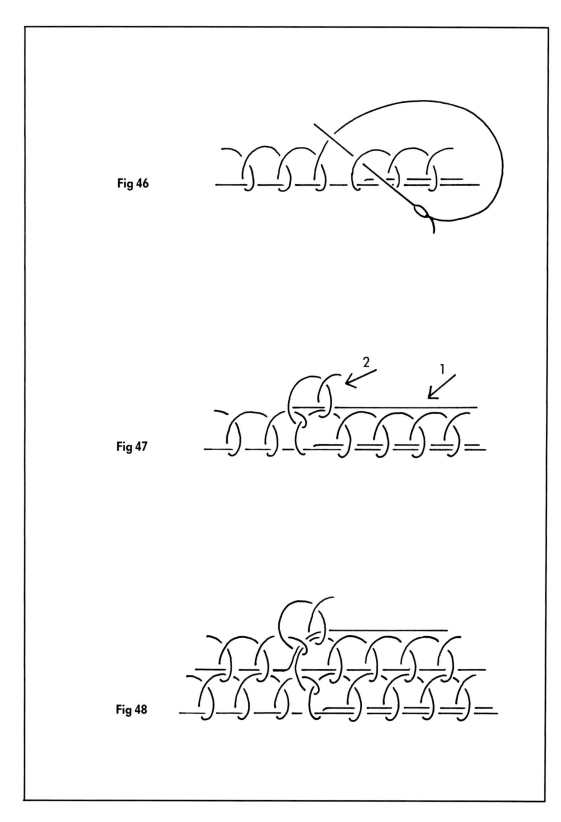

Fig 46

Fig 47

Fig 48

31

Fig 48 shows you how to work further. Make three or four rows of flatwork in the circle. When your working thread becomes too short, start a new thread in the same way as in Figs 44–45, or cut the old stretching thread. Take a new thread which is much too long in the needle. Put the needle in the last stitch working from the back to the front and make the next stitch. The part of the thread that is too long, now serves as stretching thread (Figs 49–50).

Lead the old thread with the new stretching thread over approximately eight stitches and cut the old thread. When the flat stitches reach the second traceer line (Fig 24, line 6) you have gone far enough. Cut the stretching thread and fasten every other stitch to the traceer line (see the direction of the arrow in Fig 24). When you have reached the start again, cut your thread.

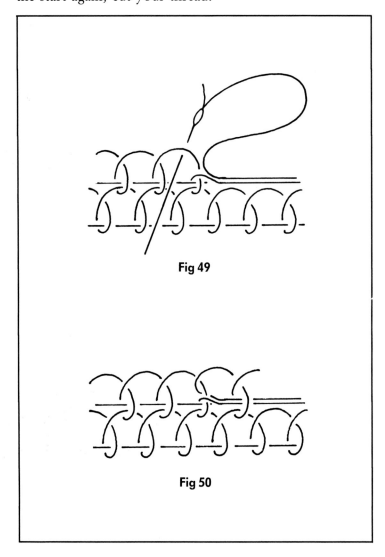

Fig 49

Fig 50

To embroider

There are two sorts of embroidery: the thin and the thick.

What is embroidery? Embroidery in Zele lace is making flat stitches over four padding threads plus the traceer line. It provides the finish.

The thin embroidery Start with *the thin embroidery* (Fig 51). Take two padding threads approximately 1 m long and fold them double. Lay the loop over **1**. Fasten these two padding threads in the loop with two stitches (Fig 52) and pull the padding threads together over the traceer line. It is very important that the four padding threads lie over the traceer line. Make a flat stitch over the four padding threads. Only take the

Fig 51

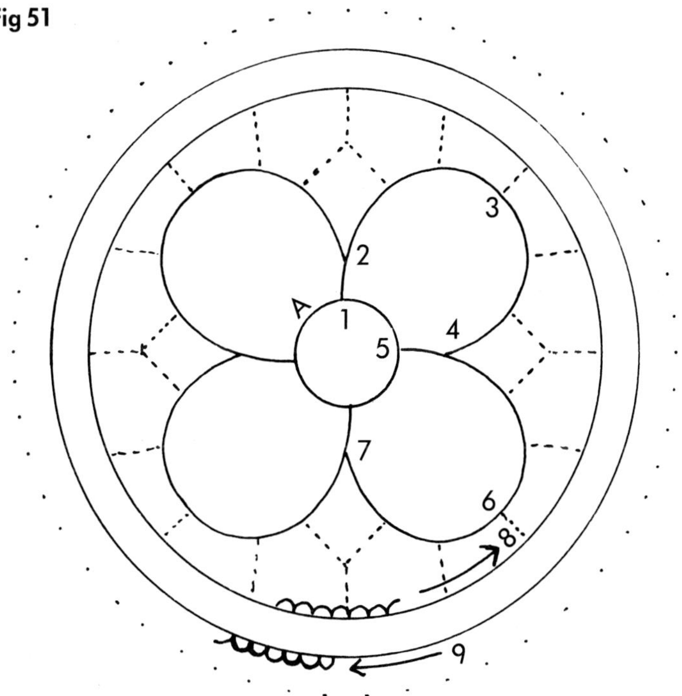

33

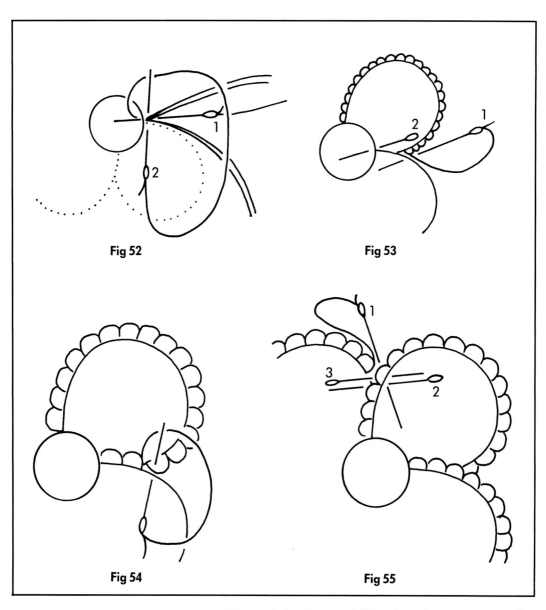

Fig 52

Fig 53

Fig 54

Fig 55

traceer line and the four padding threads on your needle. Make one embroidery stitch in every flat stitch of your filling (Fig 52, needle **2**).

Following Fig 51, embroider from **1** to **2–3** until you reach the point of **4**. Push your needle downwards under the embroidery (see the needle in Fig 53) and pull through. Push needle (no. **2**) under the traceer line at point **5**. Take two padding threads and fasten them at **5**. Pull the padding threads back to **4**, so that you have four padding threads again, and embroider from **5** to **4**. Make the embroidery above the English gaas as follows: make two flat stitches in the big spaces and one stitch in the small spaces. To make a good curve, at point **4** do not stitch completely under the traceer line, but, rather, into the middle of all the threads. Come upwards in the middle of the embroidery (Fig 54).

Embroider further in the same way. When you have reached 2 mm before point **2**, you cut the padding threads obliquely. Make sure that they are not too long or too short. Place the scissors in the middle of the embroidery in the direction 1–2 and cut the four padding threads. Embroider further until you cannot see the padding threads (Fig 55). Stick under the first embroidery as in needle **1** and come back under the embroidery, as in needle **2**. With needle **3** go back above the padding threads and under the first embroidery stitch. Finish the thread by going zig-zag under, and also in, the embroidery.

When your embroidery thread becomes too short, work as follows. Let your working thread hang. Put a new thread into the needle. Stick the needle into the last stitch from the back to the front and embroider further over six threads (the four padding threads plus the old and the new working threads). Pull the stitches a little bit tighter for about 2 cm and cut one thread. Make a few more stitches and cut the second thread.

Start on line **8** with a noose of the padding threads in the same way as at point **1**. Make a stitch in every flat stitch. Embroider till 2 mm before the end. Cut the padding threads obliquely and embroider further until you reach the connection with the first stitch.

Stick your needle in the head of the first stitch (Fig 56, needle **1**) and back under the embroidery (Fig 56, needle **2**). Finish the embroidery thread by zig-zagging under and into the embroidery. Work line **9** in the same way.

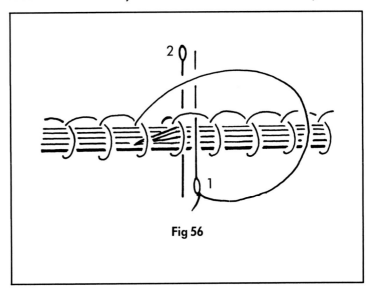

Fig 56

The thick embroidery   The little circle in the middle of the motif is worked with a thick embroidery.

Start at **A** (see Fig 51), as this is a free place. Fasten the four padding threads with an overstitch and lay them further around from **1** to **5** until you are back at **1** (see Fig 57).

Lay four padding threads over the four fastened padding threads. Now make flat stitches over eight threads, but start about 2 mm beyond the beginning and place the stitches very close to each other. Cut four padding threads obliquely about 3 mm from the end and embroider further until you reach the connecting point with the first stitch. Stick into the head of the first stitch (Fig 56). Finish the thread by zig-zagging over and again under the embroidery, and cut.

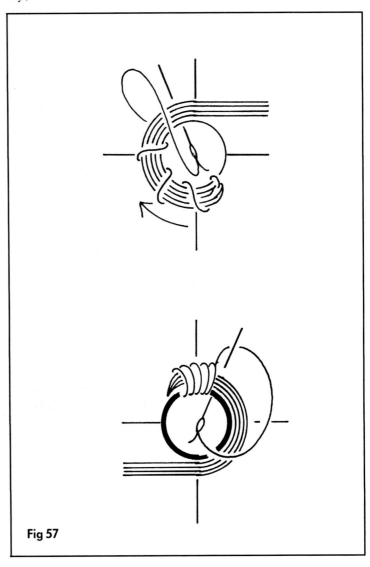

Fig 57

Photo 2: Finished motif

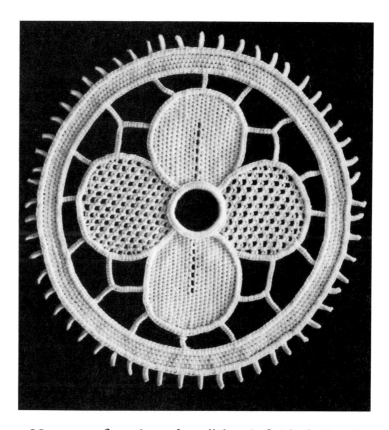

Now your first piece of needlelace is finished. Tear the two layers of cloth apart and remove the second layer of cloth from the paper. Pull all the fine threads from the underside of the pattern. When this is done, you can take the needlelace from the paper. You just have to pull out some little fine threads from the underside of your needlelace. Your first piece of needlelace is now completed.

Different forms of leaves

The simple leaf

1. Only traceer the outside.
   Start at **1**, then on to **2–3–4-5**. Take one thread to **2**. Make the connection, traceer back from **2** to **5** and fasten (see Fig 58).

2. Start with a simple leaf (see Fig 59) and look for the middle, which is also the middle vein (see the dotted line in Fig 59).

3. To work the leaf evenly in a good direction, line out the leaf, with parallel lines, from the middle to the outside (Fig 60).
   Thus you can see where you have to start working (see Fig 60 between **1** and **2**).

4. Work this leaf in the same way as in Figs 25 to 30, with flat stitch and a row of klare stitches in the middle (see Figs 31 to 35). Take care that the row of klare stitches *does not reach* the end of the leaf (see the dotted line, Fig 61).

5. You can work this row of klare stitches in three ways:
   - with a large flat stitch in the simple leaf;
   - with a twisted stitch or one stitch of English gaas in the curved leaf;
   - with a combination of both (start with a few flat stitches, near the middle use a twisted stitch or stitches, and at the end revert to flat stitches).

   It is best to work in the third way, if you have a sagging line in the middle of your leaf (Fig 62). This can help to correct and make your line straight again for the other side of the leaf.
   When you work the second half of the leaf, *make sure* that *every* stitch, at the beginning and end of the row, which forms a connection with the traceer line is fastened to the traceer thread.

6. At the end of the row work as follows: put your needle from the outside to the inside under the traceer line and *in* the stitch that connects to the traceer line. Repeat this

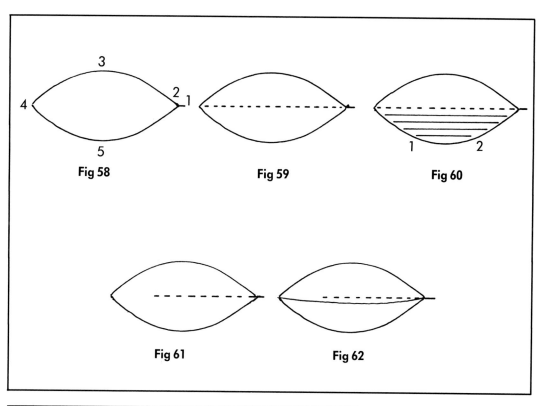

Fig 58

Fig 59

Fig 60

Fig 61

Fig 62

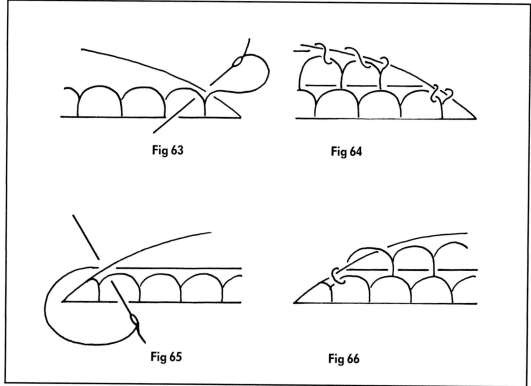

Fig 63

Fig 64

Fig 65

Fig 66

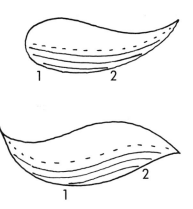

with every stitch that is connected to the traceer line (Figs 63 and 64).

7. At the beginning of the row, work as follows: lay your thread above the finished stitches as normal and bring it to the outside. Take the stitches that make connections with the traceer line and put your needle under the traceer line. In this way you can fasten your stitches to the traceer line (Figs 65 and 66). Make sure that every stitch is fastened to the traceer line so that you do not have a big space at the beginning or end of your row. In this way you can also work the leaves alongside although they are slightly curved (look carefully at the little lines). Always start at the most curved side of the leaf, between **1** and **2**.

Only embroider the outer edge.

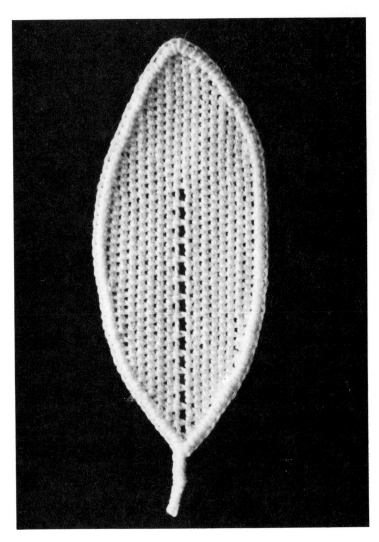

Photo 3: Simple leaf in flatwork with a row of open stitches serving as a middle vein

40

Photo 4: Simple leaf. The direction of the work is slightly curved

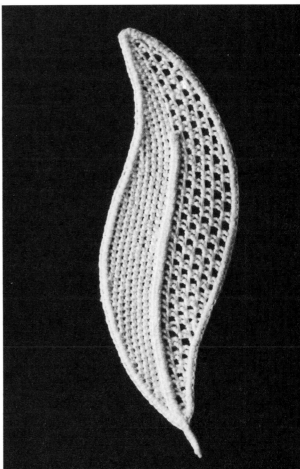

Photo 5: Simple leaf, worked in a combination of flatwork and raised English gaas (whipped twisted buttonhole stitch)

The curved leaf Traceren: Always start at the middle vein, working from **1** to **2**, with one thread to **3**. Traceer back from **3** to **2–4–5–6**. With one thread to **2**, make the connection, traceer back from **2** to **6** and cut.

Work this leaf in a different direction, to make it look a little more natural. The middle vein shows the direction of your work, but is also the *mark of division* between two parts. This means that when you have a leaf (as in Fig 67) you *always have to traceer* the middle vein and use as a *mark of division*.

When working this kind of leaf, always start at the most curved side, between **1** and **2**.

Now mark the direction for working (see the fine lines from the middle vein to the outer edge of the leaf in Fig 68).

First continue the line of the middle vein through till the point of the leaf by scoring with your needle (see dotted line in Fig 69), then line out from underneath to the upper side. As you can see, these lines *do not run parallel*: they run closer to each other at the vein than at the outer edge of the leaf.

Work this as follows. Work the first row of flat stitches as normal. Work the *first half of the second row* loose,

Work this as follows. Work the first row of flat stitches as normal. Work the *first half of the second row* loose, *work normally at the middle* and toward the vein *work stitch*). This is the only way to fill this in evenly with the same number of rows even though the space is smaller on one side.

Use the klare stitches to bring more life to your work (see the little dotted line in Fig 68). If you make a row of klare stitches and your direction does not look good, use the following guide (Fig 70). Work the row with flat stitches until the place where the vein begins, then make the vein with twisted stitches, so that it lies more open. On the way back, pick up all the large spaces and lay the thread over the flat part in the usual way. Work another row of flat stitches until you reach the vein. Take up the first large space and lay the thread back over the flat stitches. Work a new row of flat stitches, and continue it to work over the row of klare stitches.

Do not work a half row upon a normally made row just in order to correct the direction (as in Fig 71). Make sure that every stitch which connects with the traceer thread at the beginning or end of a row is well fastened (see Figs 63 to 66, the simple leaf). When you reach the top of the vein, put your needle into the noose of the traceer thread so that the vein is fastened (Fig 72).

When you have reached the top of the vein, but not the top of the leaf, work as follows:

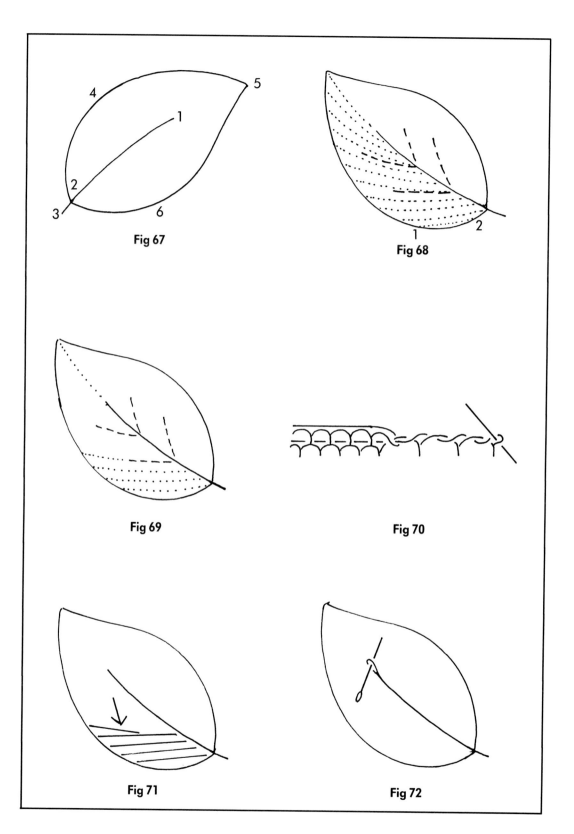

Fig 67

Fig 68

Fig 69

Fig 70

Fig 71

Fig 72

Imagine the vein is longer and work a few shorter rows on it as in Figs 73 and 74. It is better if you do not have to do this, but it is a useful trick which helps to work your leaf completely.

The other side of the leaf is a mirror image, although the lines are slightly curved (Fig 75) and you work this part from the upper to the lower edge.

If you want to work the leaf in different stitches, for example in flatwork at one side and English gaas on the other, then do as follows: pick up the last row of flat stitches at the top of the leaf (do not lay a thread). In this way you make a strong row before you change stitches.

To work stitches of different lengths on the same row, make the size of the stitch a little bit longer at the wide side and at the middle vein make one or two flat stitches. Sometimes you have to make a twisted stitch plus a flat stitch. You have to look very carefully at each row to keep a good line.

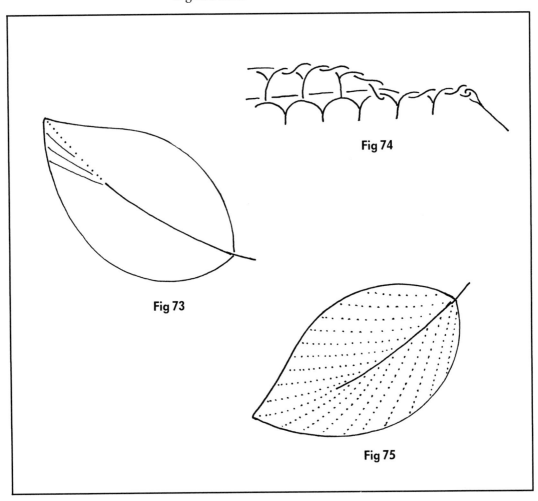

Fig 74

Fig 73

Fig 75

Leaf with a worked vein

Here we traceer only the middle vein and the outside of the leaf. Start the leaf with English gaas and work until the first vein is reached. Work a normal row of stitches up until the beginning of the vein. Take six loose padding threads and place them above the last row of stitches.

Make a flat stitch in the noose of the padding threads (Fig 76). Work the row over the padding threads with flat stitches: stitch twice in the large space and once in the small space (Fig 77). At the end of the row, you push under the traceer line and pick up every flat stitch. The following row is worked in English gaas, until you reach the next vein.

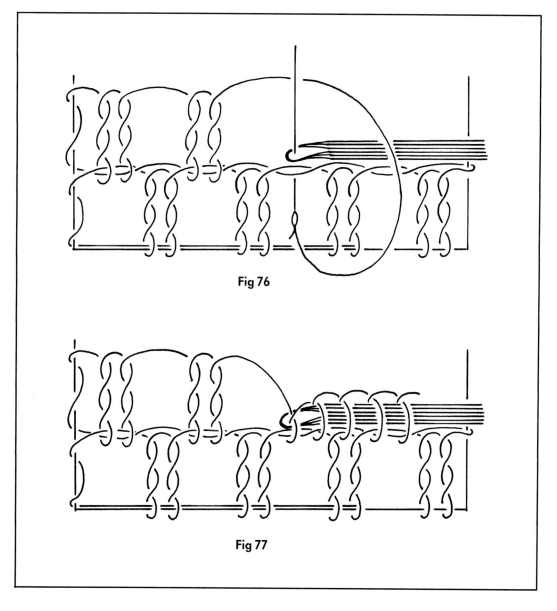

Fig 76

Fig 77

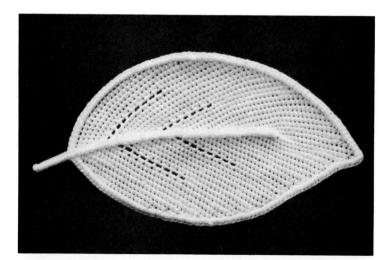

Photo 6: The curved leaf, worked in flatwork. The rows of open stitches reproduce the side veins. The direction of the work follows the leaf shape to produce the natural effect of the leaf

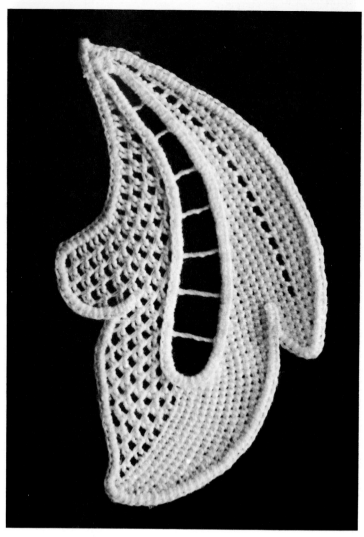

Photo 7: The curved leaf with open middle vein. This leaf contains fancy stitches (decorative stitches)

46

Photo 8: A combination of four leaves and three ways of filling

47

To decide how to embroider, you always have to look at the position of the leaf. When the leaf stands free on a stem (Fig 78) you embroider the leaf first and the vein last.

At the vein, the knots lie at the outside of the curve line. When the leaf lies in the opposite direction, you work differently. Then you embroider the vein first and the leaf last (Fig 79).

When a leaf stands over a stem, then the leaf has priority over the stem (Fig 80).

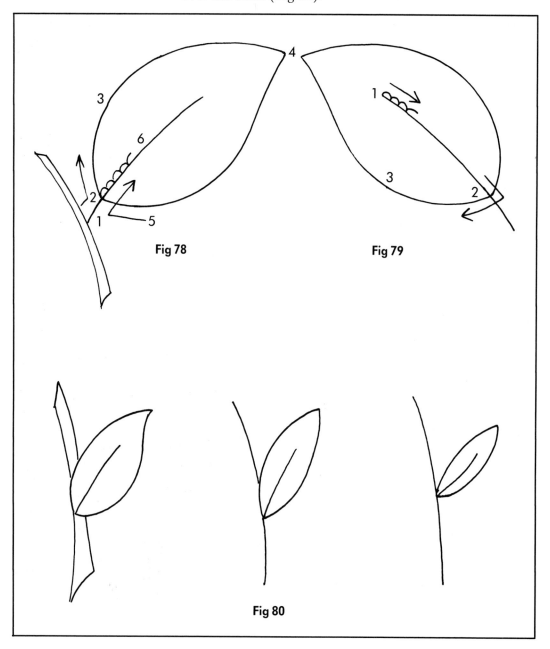

Fig 78   Fig 79

Fig 80

48

Brooch in gold and coloured
thread (worked by Clementine
Van Nieuwenhove)

Flowerpiece, worked in white cotton 100/3 by Agnes Stevens

Flowerpiece in white and gold thread (worked by Agnes Stevens)

A worked leaf, the stamens and the pearl. Also the empty rota to arrange the flowers and the leaves

Different working phases of the small leaf. From left to right: the pattern; the traceeren; the start of the work; the second half of the work; the worked leaf; the embroidered leaf

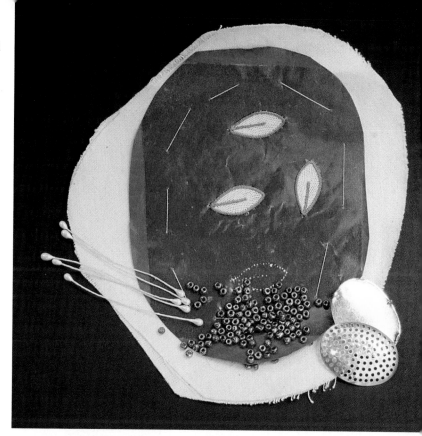

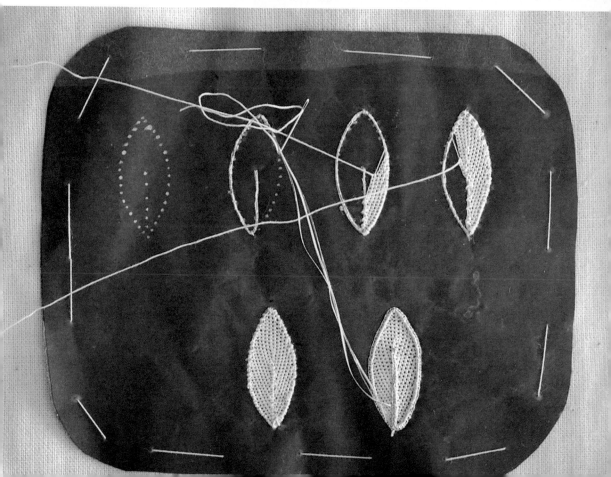

Coloured flowers on a
grapevine (worked by
Monique Buysse)

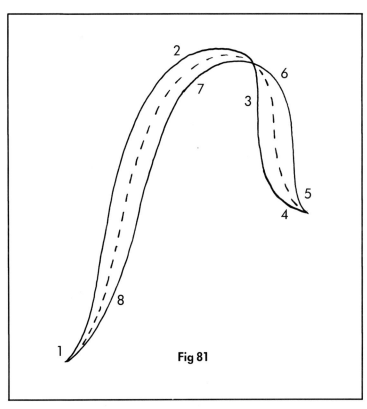

Fig 81

Leaf with shadow side   Traceer in the form of a figure eight. In this way we have a connection where the two parts of the leaf cross each other. Follow the order of the numbers (Fig 81).

If you look very carefully at this leaf, you will see two parts: the upperside and the underside or shadow side. This part is worked with shadow stitch. The working direction is the same as in the simple leaf (Fig 60). The shadow stitch is like flat stitch, but the stitches are further apart from each other, so that later on you can work two flat stitches and every big space is picked up with the stretching thread (Fig 82).

To pick out the middle vein, we use a worked vein. Work as follows: when every shadow stitch is picked up with the stretching thread, lay another six threads there and back to the end of the vein (see dotted line in Fig 81). Work over all the laid threads with a normal flat stitch. In every big opening make two flat stitches till the end of the laid threads (vein). Continue the row with the shadow stitch (Fig 83). On the return, pick up every stitch the large as well as the small stitches, with the stretching thread (Fig 84).

Continue with the shadow stitch till this part is completed. Work the upperside of the leaf with flat stitch and the middle vein with a row of klare stitches (Fig 81). For the direction of work see the lines in Fig 81.

49

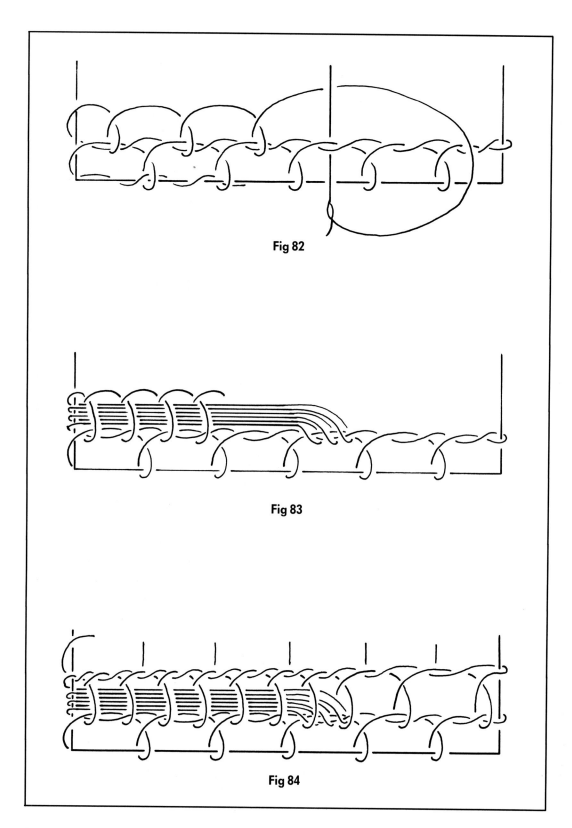

Fig 82

Fig 83

Fig 84

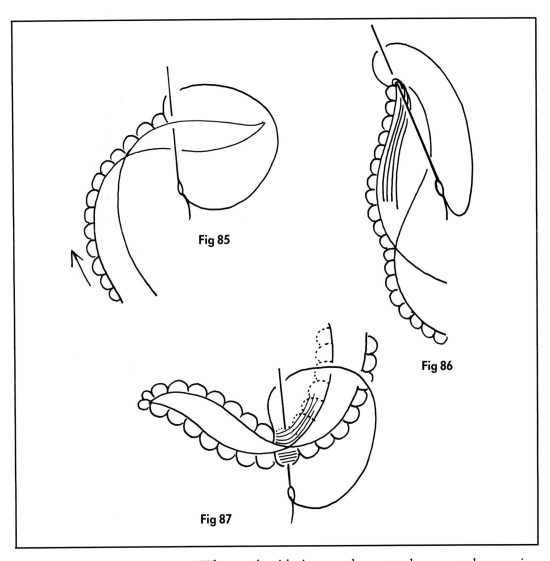

Fig 85

Fig 86

Fig 87

When embroidering you have to take care at the crossing and the point of the leaf. The full line on the design shows the correct direction of the embroidery (Fig 85).

Form the point of the leaf very carefully. Embroider up to the extreme point, fold the four padding threads so that they are parallel to the already embroidered part, and make two stitches in the point. Only then should you lay the four padding threads at their place (Fig 86) and embroider further.

At the other side, when you reach the crossing, embroider both embroidery lines. This means that just at the crossing, you take up the last embroidery but stick the needle inside of the embroidery stitch (Fig 87), so that it becomes one stitch. Stretch this stitch very carefully, and embroider to the end of the leaf.

Different brooches

When we think of a brooch, we always see the colours gold and silver. We will, therefore, try to work the following pieces of needlelace so that they can be used as real brooches.

Materials
- Fine, flat gold thread, which is used as traceer padding thread
- Three-cord gold thread for the embroidery. This triple thread will be split
- White thread no. 100/3 to work the motifs
- No. 10 Needles
- Pearls
- A backing pin for the needlelace
- Horsehair

Some general remarks
Take good care to always traceer in the same direction as for the embroidery (from left to right). Take a piece of flat gold thread, used as traceer padding thread, which is twice the length of the outline of the flower-leaf. Do the same for the small leaves.

T•E•N

Brooch

Make the traceer stitches at point **1** a little further apart from each other than usual, so that it is easy to make the connection at this point.

Using a double flat gold thread and horsehair, start at **1**, continue to **2–3–4**, over **1** to **5–6–7–8–9**. Make a connection with one gold thread and one horsehair at **1**. Traceer back from **1** to **9** and further to **10–11–12**. Make a connection at **1**. Traceer back from **1** to **12**, and further to **13–14–15**. Make another connection with **1**. Traceer back from **1** to **15** and further to **16–17**, over **1** to **18–20**. Make a connection with **5**, traceer back from **5** to **20** and finish.

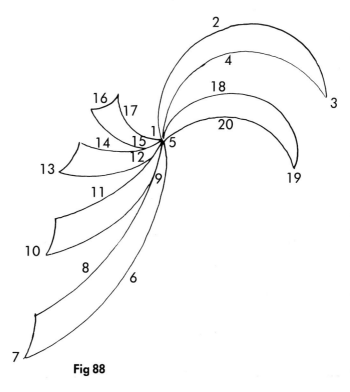

Fig 88

53

To work (Figs 89–92)   Work with thread 100/3. This brooch can be worked in different ways.

1. (Fig 89) Flatwork with a middle row of klare stitches. The dotted line shows the middle, and the fine lines show the direction of the work. Always start at the outer side of the curve (between **1** and **2**). Take care that you start and end the row of klare stitches in the same place as the dotted line. All the parts with the same shape can be worked in the same way.

2. (Fig 90) Flatwork with a row of klare stitches at the edge. You make the row of klare stitches at the inside of the curve (see the dotted line). The rest is filled with flatwork. The outlining shows the direction of the work. Make sure that every stitch which connects with the traceer line is fastened well (Figs 91 and 92). The two similar parts can be worked in the same way.

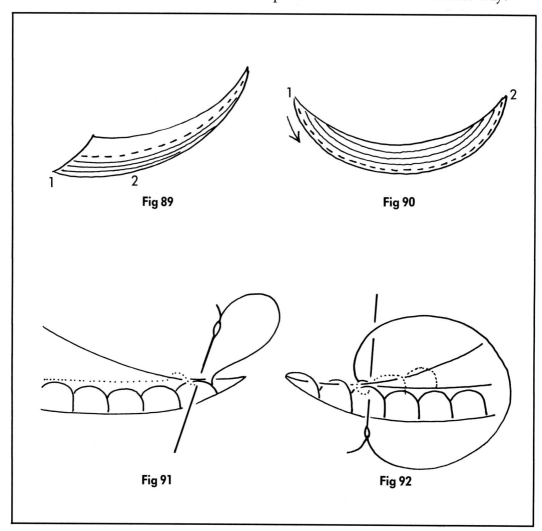

Fig 89   Fig 90

Fig 91   Fig 92

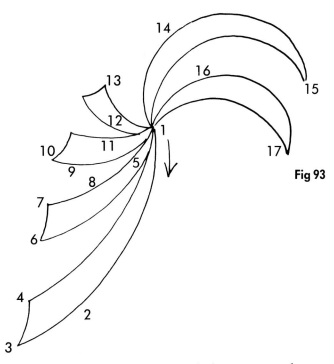

Fig 93

To embroider (Fig 93) Take a fine flat double gold thread about 150 cm long, or two fine gold threads from the three-cord thread, and a very fine gold thread in a fine needle. Make the last gold thread much too long. The extra length is then added to the padding thread.

Start at **1**. Fasten the loose ends of the padding threads very carefully. Embroider from **1** to **2** till the extreme point **3**. Turn the work so that the line between **3** and **4** is horizontal to your finger. Pull the padding threads straight back on to the next embroidery stitch to be worked and make the two first stitches of the embroidery at the line between 3 and 4. At the third stitch lay the padding threads in the normal way (Fig 94).

Embroider further till the extreme point **4**. Repeat the previously mentioned working method. At point **5** stick the needle in the opposite direction under the embroidery and go with half of the leading threads to **1** (see the first motif work Fig 53). Embroider from **1** to **5**, take up the waiting threads and embroider further to **6**. Repeat the working method used in the angles **3** and **4**.

In this way you can embroider further until you have reached the last connection at **1**. Cut off the padding thread. If your embroidery thread is still long enough, let it hang. It can be used to join up your piece of needlelace. Once everything is embroidered, you can pull your work away from the paper. First open the two layers of cloth. Remove the cloth and all those fine threads from the paper. Finally, take your piece of needlelace from the paper.

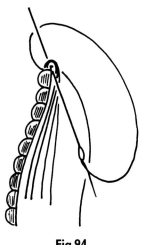

Fig 94

To join and model (Fig 95)

Bring the points **1** and **2** together and fasten them securely with the waiting thread. Fasten point **3** on top of point **1**. You can also fix a few pearls on this point with a strong thread. All that remains is to fasten everything on a pin, and then your first brooch is finished.

Fig 95

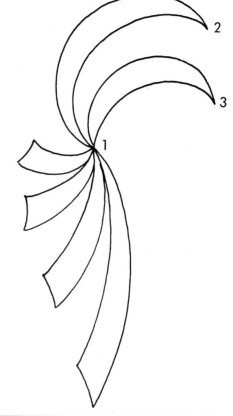

Photo 9: Brooch in Honiton thread no. 120

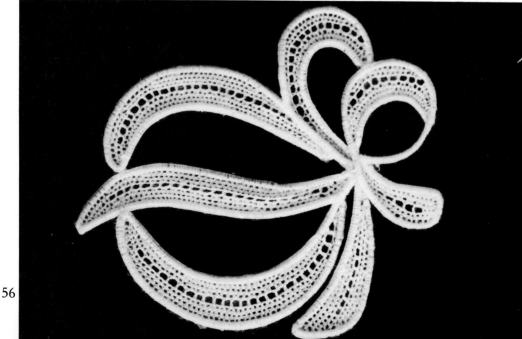

The flower brooches

These flower brooches lean towards classical work, although they look modern. You can make them up as you like:
- with large or small flowers
- with large or small leaves
- with one or more flowers, etc . . .

The petals   *Traceren*
Traceer these petals with gold thread. Make your thread long enough so that you can use it for the embroidery. Also use strands of horsehair (but not in the smallest petals). Each petal is separately traceered and worked immediately. Always start with the loose end of the padding thread at **1** (Fig 96) and further to **2–3–4** until two stitches *over* **1**. Let your padding thread hang free: you can use it for the embroidery, and cut the horsehair.

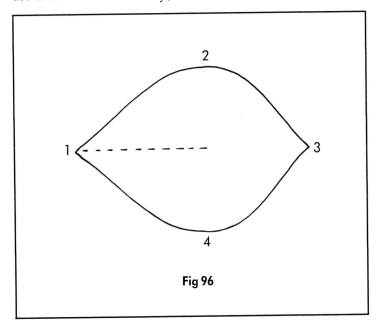

Fig 96

57

To work

You can fill up the petals in different ways, e.g.

- Flat work with a row of klare stitches which serve as a vein
- English gaas – the vein is worked and embroidered above
- Ground (ground is known as 'pea stitch' in England)

For all these stitches use the same direction of work (Fig 97). First mark the middle of the work. The fine lines show the direction of the work.

You can also fill up the petal with a row of klare stitches around the inside edge of the petal (Fig 98). This is a twisted stitch. Make sure that the stitches are parallel, have a square form and make a beautiful corner in the point. Pick up every stitch once when you turn back, even in the point. Stretch your thread well.

If you are back at point **1** and your working thread is still long enough, take your needle under **1** to the outside, bring it back and pick up the spaces for the second time till point **2**.

Start with flatwork between **2** and **3** above the row of klare stitches (Fig 99).

Photo 10: Basket with flowers, in cotton no. 60. Each flower uses a different combination of stitches. With this work I won the *Prix d'Honneur* in Le Puy (France) (Agnes Stevens)

Photo 11: Butterfly, in Honiton thread no. 120. Take particular note of the 'knots' and 'beads' in the wings. Always use horsehair to pad the outline

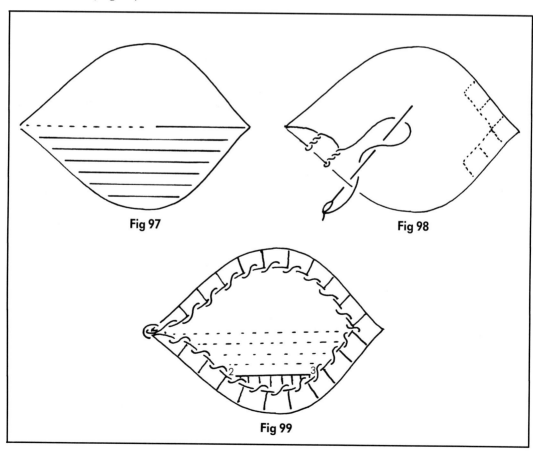

Fig 97

Fig 98

Fig 99

59

Photo 12: Hat with flowers, in
Honiton thread no. 120

Photo 13: Initials, worked in
Honiton thread no. 120

Note: as the rows get longer, you will need more stitches at the right side and at the left side you will have to stretch your laid thread further (see Figs 28–30). Also, the first piece of a new thread is laid the same way as in Fig 30. Pick out the middle vein with the row of klare stitches in flat stitches. Once you have passed the middle, the rows become shorter. Here you have to take care that every stitch which connects with the row of klare stitches is very well fastened. Work as follows (Figs 100 and 101).

The numbers of the needles give the order of the actions. Sometimes you have to repeat the action of needle **1** in Fig 100 more than once, depending on the number of stitches which connect to the row of klare stitches. When all the stitches which connect to the row of klare stitches are fastened, the next action (needle **2**) is to stretch your cording thread. Fig 101 shows the working on the left-hand side. After laying the thread on top of the stitches (needle **1**), fasten all the stitches close enough to connect to the klare stitches (needle **2**). You can only make normal stitches when your next stitch is far enough away from the row of klare stitches.

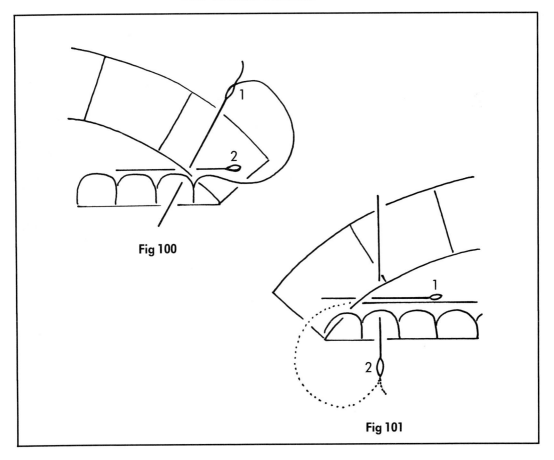

Fig 100

Fig 101

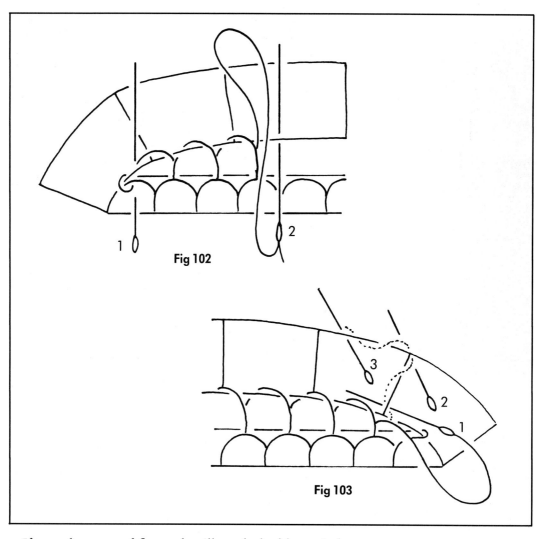

Fig 102

Fig 103

If your last row of flatwork will reach the klare stitches, you can work them straight into the klare stitches as in Fig 102.

Make sure that your laid thread is neat. Put your needle in the first flat stitch and come out *under and in* the large opening (see needle **1**). Do not make a proper stitch. *Look carefully at needle **2**, put your needle under and in the big opening and pull your thread through. Then make a normal flat stitch*. Repeat from * till * until the end of the row. Now you just have to take your thread invisibly to the outside (Fig 103). If you have worked the last flat stitch, it *is possible* that you may have *to pick up* one stitch to arrive at a leg of the row of klare stitches. Take your needle once under and around the leg and further to the traceer line. Follow in order of the numbered needles. Take needle **3** several times under the traceer line and finish.

Photo 14: Brooch worked in a combination of cotton thread 100/3 and gold thread. Only flatstitch was used.

Photo 15: Brooch: a mixture of long and short leaves. A complete flower, two little flowerbuds and a few stamens. The heart of the flower is filled with little pearls

62

Photo 16: Complete flower
with one pearl in the heart.
Under the flower are three ivy
leaves

To embroider

Add the extra length of the thread in your needle to the
two threads already hanging at the end of your petal. These
form part of the padding. Embroider the petal and take
care at the point (see working method in Fig 94). Cut the
padding threads at the end. Put your needle in the head of
the first stitch (Fig 56) and finish off the thread by
threading your needle a few times to and fro under, but in,
the embroidery. Join five petals together and fasten the
flower to the plate of the brooch. Put the flower together
with the leaves of your choice. Place a pearl in the heart of
the flower.

The leaves   *To traceer*

Traceer the leaf with gold thread and horsehair. Use the
horsehair only for the main vein and the outline of the leaf.
Start at the veins and then work toward the outside line but
in the same direction as is used for the embroidery. The
example is a small ivy leaf (Fig 104).

Fig 104

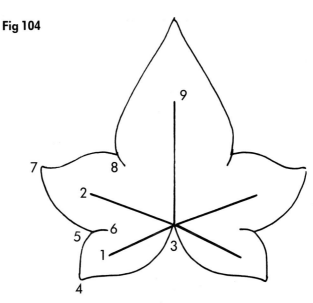

Start at the top of vein **1** with a loop of the traceer thread. Traceer from the top to the middle, go with one thread plus one horsehair to the top of vein **2** and traceer back to the middle. Continue until all the veins are traceered. Traceer further to **3–4–5**, with one thread plus one horsehair to **6**. Tracer back from **6** to **5–7–8**. Traceer further in this way till the end is reached. Cut the horsehairs and go once more over the middle vein with the gold thread. At the end, traceer two more stitches over the beginning and let the gold thread hang free until you need to embroider.

To work

It is most effective to work the leaf entirely in flatwork. It is the direction of the work that counts. In the simple leaf you can use a row of klare stitches to mark a side vein (Fig 105).

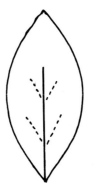

Fig 105

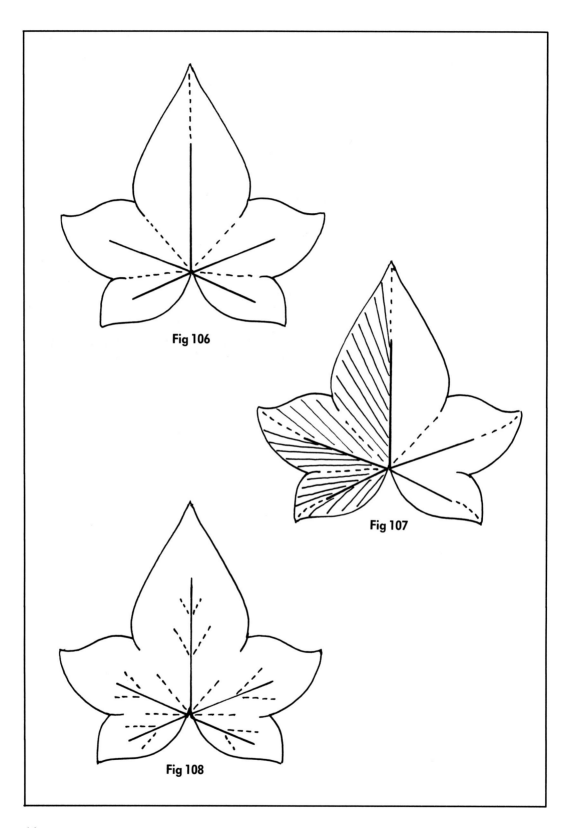

Fig 106

Fig 107

Fig 108

The dotted line shows the side vein and the fine lines mark the direction of the work. First find the basic line in your work for the ivy leaf (see the dotted line in Fig 106). Now you can see that the ivy leaf is divided into parts. Each part is a simple leaf. Outline every part like a simple leaf (Fig 107).

Now you can clearly see the direction your work should take. Do not work a row of klare stitches in the small ivy leaf: it is too small for this. But in the large ivy leaf you can work a side vein now and then (see the dotted lines in Fig 108) in klare stitches.

To embroider
If you have a gold thread hanging at the outside edge, first embroider the outside edge and then the veins. Embroider the veins in the same order as for the traceer work, so that you always end in the middle. If you have cut the gold thread at point **9**, start to embroider the veins at vein **1**, then vein **2**, *etc*. Work the outside edge last. There are various leaf and petal outlines shown on pages 68 and 69. Choose from these to make up a brooch.

Suggestions for small leaf shapes

Suggestions for petal shapes

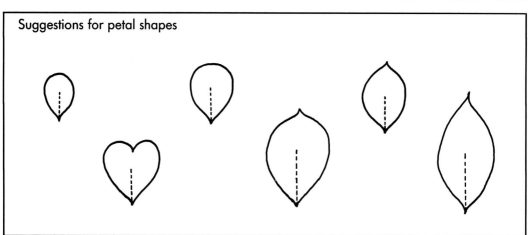

Suggestions for brooches

Suppliers

Alby Lace Centre
Cromer Road
Alby
Norwich
Norfolk

Frank Herring & Sons
27 High West Street
Dorchester
DT1 1UP

Loricraft
4 Big Lane
Lambourn
Berks RG16 7XQ

Honiton Lace Shop
44 High Street
Honiton
Devon

Mace and Nairn
89 Crane Street
Salisbury
Wilts

The Lace Guild
The Hollies
53 Audnam
Stourbridge
West Midlands
DY8 4AE

D.H. Shaw
47 Zamor Crescent
Thurscroft
Rotherham
South Yorks

John & Jennifer Ford
October Hill
Upper Way
Upper Longdon
Rugeley
Staffs WS15 1QB

Shireburn Lace
Finkle Court
Finkle
Sherburn in Elmet
North Yorks

Enid Taylor
Valley House Craft
   Studio
Ruston
Scarborough
North Yorks
YO13 9QE

George White
Delaheys Cottage
Thistle Hill
Knaresborough
North Yorks

English Lace School
Oak House
Church Stile
Woodbury
near Exeter
Devon

D.J. Hornsby
149 High Street
Burton Latimer
Kettering
Northants
NN15 5RL

Liz Bartlett
12 Creslow Court
Galley Hill
Stony Stratford
MK11 1NN

Sebalace
Waterloo Mill
Howden Road
Silsden
West Yorks BD20 0HA

T. Brown
Woodside
Greenlands Lane
Prestwood
Great Missenden
Bucks

A. Sells
49 Pedley Lane
Clifton
Shefford
Beds

C. & D. Springett
21 Hillmorton Road
Rugby
Warks CV22 5DF

B. Phillips
Pantglas
Cellen
Lampeter
Dyfed

Newnham Lane
  Equipment
11 Dorchester Close
Basingstoke
Hants RG23 8EX

Bartlett, Caesar &
  Partners
The Glen
Downton
Lymington
Hants

A L'Econome
Anne-Marie Deydier
Ecole de Dentelle aux
  Fuseaux
10 rue Paul Chenavard
69001 Lyon
France

Heikina de Ruyter
Feldohlentrup 22
4933 Blomber/Lippe
West Germany

Index